one hundred breaths later

HAYLEY STUMBO

ISBN-13:978-0692822128
ISBN-10:0692822127

Cover design by Kassi Snider, Formatting by KassiJean

Interior Formatting by Elaine York
Allusion Graphics, LLC/Publishing & Book Formatting

For the people who brought
these words to the surface.

And for Tom Petty.

inhale

BLACK AND WHITE KEYS

The piano's keys are not meant to be pressed
with anything less than your dignity.
I compose my thoughts to you
in black and white,
and I don't give you a chance to play anything else.
I will ruin the very quarter notes of this
fling
with nothing more than disappointment
that you weighted down with a tryst
you forgot to invite me to.
I will pound out my heart,
and flood your lungs with enough sand
that you'll have to write your voice from here on out.
You ask me for a hand
and how to play this coda better,
but my fingers can only play one note at a time.

OCEANS AND SEAS

When I was small
I was scared of the sea.
Of its waves and currents,
riptides,
and all the things that lived there.
And then I realized how silly it was
to be afraid of something that existed
before it even had a name.
Kind of like us.
I was terrified of you,
and of what we were to become,
before you even had the chance to drum
your fingers against my skin,
and cradle my jaw with your hands.

GIVE IT AWAY

Girls,
don't give parts of your soul
to boys who tell you "you're pretty"
while they smoke Marlboro Reds behind their
father's sheds.
Don't let them unbutton you,
sink into your veins,
and fashion an ashtray from your bones.

I READ LIKE A SCHOOL ASSIGNMENT

You were made to run
your fingers down me,
like the spine of a book,
and read aloud all the phrases
that explain the plot,
of who I am
of what I am
and why you chose to pull me
from the shelf,
dog ear all my paper-thin edges,
and hide me under your pillow for later.

SUMMER 2005

Five miles down the road,
eight feet under water in my backyard swimming pool,
that's where I spent my summer with you.
Before the cast of a shadow too light to cause shade,
I was your summertime hideaway.
Parking lot invitations,
basement rendezvous and empty small town stadiums.
I was vulnerability wrapped up in piano strings,
and I could only play by ear.
I liked to lie low on Saturdays,
weekdays were fashioned into workshops for vampire nights.
I held your hand through the finer parts of August,
        and you gave me a September to remember.
The kind of September that burns when you touch it.
There was an unforgettable scent
of guilt and shame washed between the trees.
You hang me from the lowest branch,
left me falling like leaves.
When the last hints of summer
danced through the strip mines,
I found you waiting for me by your car,
doors open,
lights on,
ready to embrace whatever ending was beginning.

ROCKS AND THINGS

I can't wait to wear you like silver,
and drip you from my neck like gold.
Next to that, we're just diamonds that
miner's hands are greedy for.
You reach for me and
twirl your fingers
in the pieces of my soul
that I leave hanging down for you to take.
You ash out your insides
with a demeanor made for
boys who love more girls than they should.
Gifting me things to keep me
gratefully quiet.
Second-handed hand-me-downs
that your last obsession neglected.
You'll do what you have to
to get me where you want to,
and I'll always want you
because I'm down with silver
and drunk on gold.

FRIDAY KNIGHT LIGHTS

Red and blue,
blue and red,
over and again.
Forced down your throat
like the rays of the sun,
when all you want is a little rain.

I never had much of a taste for color.
I've always preferred the placement of the shadows
and the lack of the spirit
flooding the hallways beyond me.

But you were the burst of color
that caused me to blow,
sprinkle into confetti,
and coat the forty-yard line.
I crawled out from under the bleachers
shaking and new,
and you pulled me up to your eye level,
kissed my forehead
and said "it's about time you showed up."

So, I never left.

GOODBYE GIRL

So, this is it?
The fireworks and all the things they told me about.
This is how it feels,
to have someone bend you
dip you and drown you
beneath them in a haze of fog.
This is what my best friend told me to call her about.
I'm sure that I rushed it,
bent its luster out of shape,
but everyone is doing it.
And I thought it'd make you keep me.

The only thing of mine you kept,
was my breath,
stained against the windows of your car.
You keyed my soul and
let me sit outside to dry.

You have a headlight out now.
You can thank me for that.

HOMECOMING

"But where are we going?"
were the only words you said
and I smiled at you from the passenger seat
and I told you "Out of our minds."

We laughed and passed the house
of the girl, you used to love.
You said you were better now,
but you wished you had found me
before the time you found her.

I smiled at the way your words laid against my chest,
tapped the fogged glass of the window,
drew a heart near the bottom
and then wiped it away when you caught me.

THE SUMMER OF POISON TREES

Poison trees bear no fruits.
except for the kind that taste sweet.
I licked the nectar of our
spoiled,
stage one
romance
off my fingers before you could
shake my hand goodbye.
From where I'm standing,
I'm drenched in shade,
and I'm fine keeping it that way.
Sometimes the summer ruins the rinds
of all the things that
I want to rip through.
My fingers blackened with the ruined fruit
of branches that dropped them before they bloomed.
The ground gathers them
and gives them to the bees.
I sink to my knees
and pray for your karma
to be much harder on you
than I could ever be.

BOYS IN BLUE

I wrote five hundred words
for you.
I gave them all to someone else
because he seemed like the kind of boy
who would help get me somewhere.
You shook your head at me,
    adjusted your tie,
      then finished your dinner with your fingers
      before finishing me off.
      I can't decide when I agreed to wear your colors,
      your number,
      your hands.
      But you pressed them against more than just skin,
      and layered them against more than just
      a journal in the top drawer.
      You ruptured the heart
      that rests beneath
      the fragments of whatever is holding it in.
      I've been plastered with newspaper clippings,
      stories I wrote but never edited,
      and tried to sell for fifty cents
      every other Friday.
      I did all these things to get your attention,
      to buckle myself into your new, old car
      and let you drive me home
      because it was on your way.

NORTH FOR THE SUMMER

I carved rivers into mountains,
so you could swim instead of climb.
But you pulled at me,
like an anchor cuts through the sea,
And sinks to the floor below.

So, I made roads for you,
And I paved them with good intentions and dreams you often
carried.
But you told me you'd rather walk through deserts,
And bake in the Nevada sun.

I carved out my soul for you,
with a rusty spoon that used to hang on my wall as a decoration.
You just laughed and asked if there was anything else to do in this
town,
because you were bored with all that surrounds you.

I gave my smile to you,
on a whim when I was knee deep in tonic and a cheap, brown rum.
You pocketed it neatly next to your phone,
and promised you'd call me in the morning.

I lost part of who I was inside of you,
waiting around for you after you disappeared from sight.
They told me you moved, headed North for the summer,
and I never saw you again.

ONE HUNDRED BREATHS LATER

He told me to count down from one hundred to zero
and with each number to take a breath.
He said that in time,
I would forget about breathing,
it would become a habit.
The lesson was to teach me to let life happen,
let things go until they become second nature.
To cope with the thoughts of a too-clouded mind,
and to find some solace without the aid of a drug.
So, I began to count down
and one hundred breaths later
I was out of numbers and ways to forget about things,
to forget about him.

And I still remembered it all.

BLACKTOP SONGS

The blacktop sang to me even though I was deaf,
I was void of all sound that had nothing to do with you.
Yet it moved beneath my feet and begged me to dance,
so I moved effortlessly against it and followed the lines of parking
spaces.
You caught me then, and whistled in my ear,
told me it was time to go home.
On the way, we passed the barn that smiled
and the road that led to the empty fields,
and you gave me a look that begged me to trust you.
So, I did.

I trusted you forever even back then.
No words,
no sound
just the feeling of fingers on shaking skin.
Bones turned to ash at the thought of us breaking each other.
I let you devour me,
and I asked you to do it again.

But even blacktop loses its color,
and the cracks in sunburned tar separate the parking lot into pieces.
Time stretched on and days became weeks,
weeks passed months and went straight to years.
I asked someone else to devour me,
I told him about that very spot,
he drove through the field with his lights off.
The entire time he spoke to me,
but I was deaf again.
Void of all sound that wasn't you.

I pretended his hands were yours.
I begged his lips to stain me the way yours had done so long ago.
I cried when I realized he loved me,
because you never did.

They repaved that parking lot,
hid all the cracks,
dug up the old pavement and re-laid my life.
It no longer sings,
no longer holds any part of what I used to be.
I still hear nothing.
Deaf.
Void of all sound that isn't you.

ALMOST

This is the soundtrack to the fall.
The first snow coated your mother's new driveway
and you told me you couldn't wait to show me the winter.
I swallowed your lies before they reached your teeth.
I perched myself by your dining room table,
and let your sister convince me to stay until the weather let up.
You gnawed your cheek
and disappeared to the lower level,
while I looked around one final time.

You and I were merely over,
but we were still wearing the façade of almost-somethings,
to appease our surroundings.
I knew we were exiled,
but I drank you in as I ground my soles into your carpet.
I swore to myself I'd never let you forget me,
and I left a trail of bones through your room.

We'd come full circle,
and I'd never trust something that has no edges.
I took a right out of your life and wrapped my car around a tree.
Totaled,
and equally wrecked.

I don't feel you anymore.

KEEP YOUR HANDS TO YOURSELF

I know that you've seen all the ways my body bends,
and I know you have places you like to place your hands,
but I'd like it more if you loved me
the way you loved her
on Thursday afternoons.
Do you still feel at all?
Or do you just beat on,
thumping out of habit,
living out of score,
because you can't settle whatever you two have?
You're the cake at a wedding
that never gets sliced,
but somehow you end up in all the pictures
and on the plates of the guests who were invited
out of circumstance.
    I keep seeing you everywhere.
You crack me while you crack up
and split me right down the middle.
I catch you dancing with the girl you brought,
your hands lace in hers before you find the spot next to me,
that's empty.

BURNT

You burnt me out like Christmas lights,
that flicker into mid-April
And hang from branches of trees.
Tress that have
not
yet
blossomed
or given up their frost.
Still I hang loosely,
hoping to light up the evening again.
If only someone remembers
to change me.

ONE FIFTY ONE

Step into my office, you said,
as you dangled her in front of me like a trap.
You clearly wanted a reaction,
all I wanted was to remember who I used to be.
Before you.

Seven hours is a long time to travel with someone who ruined you,
it's hard enough waking up in the morning and living through the day.
We stopped in Chicago, near Navy Pier,
and you pointed out the frozen lake and how it made you feel empty.

Three days was all it took to fall back in love with you.
Three days.
To eat my plateful of regrets and make you a habit again.
I buried that hatred inside of myself and forced a smile when I saw you.
It worked because you looked at me,
not once but twice,
and we planned to meet each other when the city died down.
(Cities don't ever die down.)

"Tell me I'm pretty."
Four words that I wish I could swallow back down.
But I didn't,
and you did.
I fell over my feet and into your side one.
You said,
"Listen to this song, it reminds me of us."
And regardless if it was melodic,
or just bursts of sound,
I melded into the vapor pressing off your lungs,
that coated your lips with lies.
I was a goner.
I collapsed at the thought of us and you carried me to bed.

I spent the night on a tiled floor,
begging you to keep me warm.
You didn't, but then again, what's new?
There is not a touch from someone warm
that could begin to thaw me out.
Not after this.

DECEMBER 31, 2006

I spent my New Year's Eve in the bay of a car wash,
ringing it in with people who didn't care
what my resolutions were
or if I kept them.
I followed your lead
to a party near the edge of town
and I kept myself out of the picture.
In between plastic cups and cigarettes I shouldn't have smoked,
you asked me how it felt to fly,
and what happened to us.
I still don't have an answer for why we halted mid-year,
but I wanted you back.
I wanted back what was mine.
I took it, with needy fingers
and a needle point love
that would be gone by morning anyway.
The snow was soft, the type that should have melted
but the temperature dropped and kept it around.
Just like you and me.
A lingering allergy to an old bit of lust,
that was thrown out and should have been left there to rust.

SERPENT TURPENTINE

We used to trade fires for Boone's Farm and beers,
sit in plastic chairs and pretend
this was growing up.

Those fires grew wild and raged.
People would come home for the summer and catch some of the
sparks,
and one of those sparks caught you.

I'm still not sure what I was thinking,
maybe I thought you were a safety net
something I could catch myself in but be okay with.
I was wrong.

You unwrapped me and let me dry out.
I no longer burned with the taste of another,
instead I was captivated with whatever poison you were telling me.

I let you slither into my soul like a snake,
and you stayed there
far longer than you should have,
shed your skin,
outlived your welcome,
and never did have the courtesy to put me back together again.

GONE

I am as restricting as caution tape,
draped across a crime scene in a small town
where nothing ever happens.
I keep you out minimally
but you still creep inside
and laugh at my failed attempts
to block the door.
How could anyone blame you?
The boy who is going places,
all the places I'll never be.
I should be so lucky
to be in your company.
But what if I never wanted you?
What if I was content with
treading through water?
Maybe I didn't need someone to guide me,
to introduce me to the finer parts of life,
the parts where last names
are everything.
I am okay with being so unimpressive
that no one wants to try me out.

TWO STAIRCASES

I climbed two sets of stairs
only to find that they both led
to the room at the top,
the one you slept in for a while.
There was no growing up,
just going down into your bones
and staying warm there through the winter.
Your twin sisters bit their silver tongues
every time I stopped over to visit,
because everyone knew the real reason
I was there,
had little to do with our friendship,
and more to do with your hold on me.
I should have been in the basement
but instead I was climbing to attics,
and hanging myself off the awning over your porch.
I cut the corners
of your edges and
sliced my fingers on blades of grass
that grew beyond your bedroom window.
Wherever it is you're going,
I wish you well wherever you end up.
I used to wonder how you lived with yourself,
now I wonder how I ever wanted to live with you.

DIRTY

You were the splash in my pool of growing up.
I never told you how much I relied on your life,
to come and pull some from my bones.
We spent too much time
in treehouses and cars,
but I learned the best tricks that way.
Like how to drive a yard
with a bucket of sand,
and how to drag a lake
with nothing more than your fingers.
In the hammock of your bedroom,
you told me
"this is how you grow up"
and you promised to grow with me.
Next to all the things we would become,
and all the boys that we would love.
You told me one would gut me and I would learn how to bleed,
in my time of growing I didn't believe a word you said.
But you knew it all, even back then.

exhale

SOMETIME IN FEBRUARY 2007

I've got such an envious heart;
It sloshes and aches
when you touch her face,
and I don't know what to do with it,
other than to just
let
it
break.

THAT TIME WE ALMOST BEGAN AGAIN

You almost got away with it,
the feeling of your hands on my face,
I mean.

I almost caved in.
You could have had me
on top of the roof,
bright and warm under Cassiopeia
and all her vain thoughts.

Instead we talked until the sun tilted her from our view,
you told me about how your life has been
since I've been gone from it.

You laughed and asked me about Margo;
about how she has been.
I told you I didn't know who Margo was,
you shrugged your shoulders
and told me you had me confused with someone else.

LANE AND HIGH

I took myself to a new place
with the hopes of starting fresh.
All my wounds had closed,
the scars white against summer's leftover tan.
I cut my hair and shed my skin,
made a plan on how to live forever,
and choked down stale beer
with a girl who didn't know what she wanted to be.
I wonder what she did become
or if she is still where
Lane meets High
struggling to figure out who she is,
in an endless land of leftovers,
and empty green bottles that someone gave her
when he ran out of promises.

TWO-A-DAYS

The places I'm from are speckled all over me,
decorated for weekends
and cleaned for company.
I'm blue like the sound of a Bob Dylan song,
and sometimes I wish that you knew how to sing.
I let your eyes do the explaining,
let them skim out a story and
follow my fingers
while they trace the neck of a guitar
and strip away the afternoon.
There's a sweetness on the breeze
dipped in summertime honey,
the raw kind from the hives
where all the rich kids hide.
Somewhere near the field house,
you're knee deep in
two-a-days,
trying to pretend like that would give you
something worth bragging about.
The pines block our view,
but we still linger longer,
looking for a sign of what you're made of.
You throw yourself into an August rush,
and I can see the ghost of how you'll spend your evening
creep across your chest as you run.
My lips are sour,
bathed in lemon juice and despair,
and all the while I try to sweeten them,
you continue to make me pucker and pout.

LOVE IS RICH

Chandeliers and champagne dances,
some of the best romances of my life,
    all started by mistake.
    You belonged to another,
    I was free,
    chained to my life of imagination,
    but you wanted reality to come take ahold of me.
    You grasped me with a grip
    meant for Swisher Sweets and steering wheels.
    I'm a loose cannon,
    I'll blow you up and away
    without concern,
    but I will cry over your loss
    and empty myself for days.
    I'm not worth a prayer
    or even a drop of tonic in your gin,
    but I'll get under your skin
    the way you bedded yourself into mine.

ANCHORS OFF THE BOW

If I put you underwater
and anchor you to the ocean floor,
you would still find a way
to pull me from the sky,
and dip me into the depths with you.
That's just how you do.
You row like an oar through the
veins of my soul,
and maybe that's where you're supposed to be.
Tearing through me.

I'M YOUR GHOST

I don't want you to leave marks on my neck,
but at least then she'll know where you've been.
I feel like a villain strung out from too much good,
begging for a dash of salt
to throw in my wounds.

Your biggest mistake,
is the one you made,
when you had me stay over because I was too drunk to drive,
too tired to sleep,
and too in love with you to argue.
You are superior at getting me,
right where you want me.

SMALL TOWN TELL ALL

I guess there isn't much to say about this anymore.
Everyone knows "everything"
Every detail and disorder
and I and you,
and the things we went through
and how to make this story shorter.
We are the shame on the faces of parents
who can't believe they let their kids
run around with the likes of us.
We are the lean in the bodies of the fans
at Friday night games
as they whisper our stories
to the rest of the crowd.

I am sick of being
ample and able,
yearning for you to come back to me.
I am tired of being
the name on the tongues
of all the people I don't like.

I will stick to where I'm standing,
and I will play my game
beneath every word you threw at me.

RUN, BABY, RUN

You suck the life out of me,
Just so you can bed my soul.
I comply.
Because there's nothing more daring than you,
even if I'm not yours,
I dare someone to try to pry my hands from you.
I'll take whatever I can get.
I'll take you pretending not to notice me,
while I laugh loudly on purpose with your cousin,
who invites me over to your family's lake house later.
You raise your eyebrows and I sense your reluctance.
Here I am pressing myself into your life
and there's little you can do to stop it.
I show up,
you leave because you've got a girlfriend now,
and you make sure I know that as you glide by me.
I don't really mind your absence,
I'll still stain every ounce of your belongings
with all the things you did to me.
You come home as I'm leaving and you stop me in the garage.
You tell me to quit showing up in your life.
I tell you to quit falling back in love with me.
You ask me what I want and I hesitate,
"Cut to the chase"
and I just run away,
right before you get the chance to run your fingers down my face.

LEFT AND LESS

I'll stop writing about you
When you decide to stop hanging around,
Leaning against the fence posts of my heart
Like you've been waiting for me all along.
Don't make me the bad guy,
Not this time anyway.
I loved you when you wanted to leave,
And I loved you when you left.
But after a while I grew sick of your phantom heart.
And all the phone calls when you became bored
With a winterless February.

SOUVENIRS

Shake me like a snow globe
That you picked up at a souvenir shop
To remind you of places
That helped shape you when you were young.
If I don't make you yearn for your youth,
Sell me at your yearly yard sale,
And let me mean something to someone else.
Okay,
I'd forgive you,
even after you forgot about me.
You shake me up just to break me down.
And dammit, I can be beautiful when I want to.

FREQUENTLY FREQUENTED

I'm stuck in the corner of a bar we used to frequent,
and from where I'm sitting,
it seems that you must frequently replace me,
with somebody else.
I swirl my vodka tonic,
two limes on the rim,
and suck down all my temptation through the thin black straw
they gave me as a stir stick.
I tap my hands on the lacquered wood and
blow you a one-fingered kiss.
Finding out
that you're going out
with somebody else,
would have been better over the phone.
But you can't see me from here,
And I love the view of this mid-thirty-year-old divorcee and you.
I couldn't make this stuff up.
I order you both a drink and it's delivered to you on the house.
You clink your glasses,
whisper something in her ear,
and all the dive bars in all the small towns,
burn down at the thought of your forever.

TANGERINE

The words were always wrong.
No matter how many times we looked them up,
we sang the wrong verses
and hummed the wrong melodies.
But, oh well.
Because I loved your off-beat harmonies,
Mixed with lyrics that made no sense.
All of that reminded me of us.
A sweet disaster,
catastrophe.
You were exceptionally well versed
with skimming your fingertips across my skin,
while you tapped them in time
and in tune
with the music cutting through the speakers in your car.
Your backseat was coated with junior varsity oddities,
trophies from games you never played,
and bags of clothes in case you made it back to practice.
But we weren't going anywhere,
you made that clear when your lazy grin found a twin in my own.
Kindred spirits,
or something like that.
Your breath on my face
winded the breath in my chest.
"I'm your yellow,
                    and I'll turn you red."

THE GIRL WHO KNEW TOO LITTLE

The worst thing I ever did,
was give a piece of myself to a boy
who loved another girl.
He loved her with a flame that smoldered,
long after his fingers had stained her skin.
He loved me for all the wrong reasons,
and when he went home at night,
he'd call her and tell her
all about me.
I was nothing more than revenge cake,
he took bites from me often,
And licked his fingers afterwards.

THE EYE OF THE HURRICANE

The truest love I ever found
came when everything else was leaving.
it tore through me like shrapnel,
and I fused myself to its warmth.
A hurricane.
The kind that never calms,
no matter where the eye settles.
When you blew away,
you didn't take me with you.
I was left in the wake of disaster,
stripping boards off the windows of my soul,
and setting my bones back in place.
How appropriate it is to be blessed with
love
when nothing loves you back.

YOU'LL STOP AT NOTHING

My life started the night you climbed through a window
just to get to me.
Your parents didn't trust you when they were out of town,
so they pick-pocketed your way into the house
of a friend of a friend,
And you lasted there until the lights went out.
Did they really think you'd stay?
As if adult supervision could keep a boy in lust in.
I'll never forget the way your shadow crept in
when you finally made it to the edge of the trees.
　　　Was I worth all this trouble?
　　　　　I am worth all this trouble.
You met me where the streetlights curved like ribs
and ignited enough of the intentions on your face,
that I knew where things would be going.
I could see your breath in the air.
I could feel your breath on my skin.
　　　You could be ruined for this,
　　　　stripped from the team and out for a season,
　　　　"but I really don't care."
　　　　　"You're worth all this trouble."
I was worth it for about the ten seconds it took you to grow tired
of me.
I found trouble in the form of longing for your attention.

ROUND ROOM

It's like spinning on a carousel;
Unnecessary,
yet worth talking about later,
just so you can say you've done it.
But the world's already moving.
I'm already dizzy.
You're already too old
for amusement like this.

SHAME, SHAME

With every bounce of the ball at half court,
your eyes moved to mine.
I shouldn't be here,
but I showed up,
to show off
what you did to me.
I find comfort in your worry,
over the fact
that you left marks on my neck
    for everyone to see.
She spotted me at halftime,
and she threw you some ice
that she'll spoon feed you later,
after you've single-handedly lost the game,
and every single plot
to the stories you planned to tell her,
of where you were last night.

Good luck digging your way out of this one.
I'm still in the callouses of your hands,
right where you left me.

hold your
breath

PANTHER'S HOLLOW ROAD

I think I tried to like you, because I wanted to ruin her.
I drove the thirty-mile chip seal drive
with a Marlboro Menthol Light
clenched between my teeth.
When I pulled up your parents' incline,
you told me they were gone for the evening,
and we had the place to ourselves.
We still never left your garage.
I can't even remember what we did,
other than ash out our insides,
and talk about the way the girls in high school made you feel
sick in your own skin.
You showed me around your yard,
a tour for someone who wasn't planning on ever coming back,
and before I left,
you leaned in,
blew smoke across my face,
and kissed me too softly that I wasn't sure if I felt it.
I left in a hurry and stumbled my way home.
I smoked three cigarettes and delved my fingers into my lips
to make sure they weren't numb.
I came back fourteen times before the weather turned bad.
You were the most intimate thing I've ever felt,
and you never even touched me at all.

POOR YOU

Your friends want to know why
you called it quits,
and you can't give them a reason enough,
to be a reason at all.
You let the rise and fall of your shoulders do the talking,
and I let the sound of a mediocre excuse roll from my tongue
and attach to my cheek.
But you don't bother picking at my skin,
instead you drive home and leave the details
to your fingers
when they punch out your desires for later.
I throw on a jean jacket
and do my best to look like I didn't plan this,
but I've been waiting for you to ring me all day.
I let you do the talking,
and make the first move,
then I sit in your car and try to remember what it felt like to be yours,
not just the girl who's easy for you to knot.
I'm that spare change in your console
you keep but never spend.
Emergency dimes
for emergency times,
when you can't use your charm as currency.

AFTERWARDS

I think the hardest thing I endured with you,
were the nights I spent flanking your side,
because we had the same friends
and frequented the same places.
I had to watch you fall in love
with a handful of other girls,
who weren't me.
I was always around,
feeding off your once in a lifetime
whirlwind romances
with all the pretty girls.
It became harder to let you go
especially knowing that I didn't have the grip to hold onto you.

FRI(END)S

Five sinking words that will drown you in cement,
We
       Can
            Still
                Be
                     Friends.
Friends.
Like it's bait you'd dangle in front of me,
Something to appease that empty spot in my chest.
But friends don't do these things to each other.
There's no back and forth,
Left and right,
"where are you going to sleep tonight?"
Followed closely by the sound
Of your lips on another,
Your hands on her waist,
And then I'm slowly fading to the background.
You start to not even be able to look at me.
I blind you and you make the ground
A place to bed your eyes,
Which gives your body a break from her.
I dug our
     "we can still be friends" demeanor
Out of the ground
With brittle fingers and a feather for a shovel.
Needless to say,
It didn't get me too far.

YOU RUINED 18

Attic apartments are no places
for relationships to begin.
Garage parties in college towns are no better,
and it would have been smart of me to just stay home.
You were hungry for a full time
one-night stand,
and a part-time girl with a taste for flings.
Instead, you got a girl with enough love to fill a room,
and that was too much.
Jack and Coke.
Tequila slings.
Camel Crushes on that built-for-one deck,
and cold fingers in your dorm room bed.
Whatever it was,
it was over before my ashes hit the ground,
and your boots crushed the filter.
I chased the smoke through a year of my late teens
with hope for better twenties.

LOCKER ROOM TALK

I was the mess that created the fall-out
and your first fight
with your new girlfriend.
I did it on purpose,
Force fed the stories I'd heard
to the boys I knew would tell them to you,
in the locker room at halftime.
I did it out of spite,
I had no other reason to click my heels
and ruin your affair.
I came home from school for this;
To watch the show go down.

ROMEO 2K08

He threw rocks at my window once,
long after our candle had burnt
at both ends.
He said he needed a place to stay,
just for the night,
just for the day.
But I didn't hear the stones hit the glass.
I wasn't even home.
I was too busy trying to fill the void he left,
overcompensating for the hole
shot through my life.

I've got this feeling that if I had caught your stones,
and kept them in a drawer
to use as weapons later,
I would have found myself
throwing them at your best friend's window,
just to let you know how it feels,
to have someone else feel me.

THE AGE OF I DON'T LOVE YOU

This is the age of
"I don't love you"
And it stings like a hornet with a taste for honey.
Line drying like clothes
on a monsoon Saturday,
when the forecast only called for shade.
violet and violent
the church bells won't even ring,
and instead we've been given a siren.
You're parched for a drink
you didn't know you needed,
and you search for a way to make one gulp last all day.
But even thirst can quench itself.
So I became the glass of water on your bedside table.
The one you never drink,
but leave there in case you
wake up thirsty.
I stain the wood,
and leave a ring where I've been.
Your mother yells at you about it later,
but you can't buff out something
that was never meant to not be seen.

GREENHOUSE

On tip-toes I rise
to meet the false hope in your eyes,
and I suspend myself from your chest.
You set me in place
with a padlock heart
and you can't find the key to open my ribs.
A skeleton key that will open any door
but won't do a damn thing for a hungry soul.
Your hands are vines,
the creeping kind,
and they linger too long and too lazily against my ribs.
If you're going to take my breath away,
please make it quicker than this.
You slam the doors of houses that aren't your home,
with no explanation why
I mean so little to you.
I stay under the patchwork quilt for hours,
waiting for the sun to burn my skin,
and choke on the thought of having to face everyone
who knows what we did last night,
alone.

And all at once I realize,
This isn't how people are supposed to treat me.
So I just run.

BROKEN BREAK

"We just need to take a break"
on us
on love.
But breaks are for bones,
or nine to fivers,
and you just shook your head and walked home.
I stumbled around the curbs by your neighbors,
and decided maybe you were right,
and I fell into the whispered part of my life.
Nothing much changed,
there were kisses and dates,
and this easygoing feeling of you spending time with other girls,
and me walking home with other boys.
We do that as girls,
let boys have the easy way out,
when all we want
is someone to go easy on our hearts.

FALSE INTENTIONS

There's something about the rattle of cymbals
that bends my heart out of shape.
I suppose it has something to do
with the way you skim the metal
and forget everything going on around you.
I befriended your college girlfriend
on the hopes that it would get me closer to you.
She invited me over after your show,
and I stood on her porch and smoked all your cigarettes,
then threw my lipstick-stained filters across the chipped floorboards.
In peering through the frosted windows
I snuck a peek at your life together,
and you dropped your arm from her shoulder
when you caught me looking in,
as if I was still your Saturday night special.

So I guess that's where we begin again.

MESSAGES IN BOTTLES

How perfect it is
that the pieces of me I've bottled for you,
now safely ride
in the glovebox of your car,
right above your new girlfriend's
cut-off shorts.

And when you pull into her driveway
and drop her off,
while her mother watches from the upstairs window,
you cop a feel.
Hands on her knees,
she thinks you mean every touch.
You brush her lips with your thumb,
and tell her you'll see her tomorrow.

On your way home,
you turn up your radio
and frown because the song reminds you of me.
You glance in the rearview mirror,
shocked
to find me smiling in your backseat.
You make a left,
down the hill,
and crash into my garage
Because I'm home alone again.

EMPTY LIKE THE BED

The coldest I've ever been,
was after a kiss
before a call
to the girl you should have been spending the night with.
You snuck into the kitchen just to tell her
"I love you"
then came back to me,
and took off your shirt.

I heard every word,
But I let you use me,
once,
twice,
and then you called her and told her goodnight.

I let you curl up next to me,
and press your bones into mine.
A perfect fit for someone
        who needs a room
for a place to store
all the terrible things he's done.

IRON-LUNGED BEAUTY

My chest is full of hawks,
swooping and diving,
picking at the bones and pieces I've left for the sun.
My chest often aches,
when you lay your hand upon it,
palm open,
eyes closed.
My chest is made of metal,
a fortress you can't spear.
With these iron lungs, I learned to breathe,
spit out your polluted words,
and clambered my way down the ladder of your soul.
My chest heaves at the thought
of breathing without you,
but I cough up water
and it spills at your feet,
I let it do the flooding and I
carry on.

YOU, ME, WE

You.
You were meant to bask in the glory
of another ruthless summer,
where you just coast on without me.
Me.
I was meant to sail across the sky
with the hope of hanging myself up
on the back of a bird or the branch of a tree.
We.
We crashed into each other,
my cape, your boat,
and you didn't care for that very much.

I never wanted to coast through life.
I've always been hungry for mountains and waves.
Let me float along with twitching fingers.
I'll be fine,
until I'm not.
And then I'll dive.

You.
You will try to save me with your net,
even though you didn't really want to catch me any way.
Me.
I'll be fine,
until I'm not.

THE GLEAMING

I hate that I can always find you in my closet,
under my shoes and sweatshirts.
I hate that you gleam when I notice you
noticing me.
I guess I should be grateful for whatever it was we dipped into.

I often forget that there's a time in our life
where we stopped knowing each other's favorite things,
and swiftly became strangers.

From being the very blood in my veins,
to walking past me,
pretending that you can't see my eyes
as they struggle to see anything else but you.
I pull myself off your mind,
right before you ink yourself into mine.
We are the echoes of all the things we never meant to say,
under a bridge,
behind the sky.
It's easy to forget someone,
when they forget to love you.

YEARS AFTER

At some point you have to give up the grudge,
and I planned to.
I planned to say hello, like a kind stranger.
We're older now,
not so rough around the edges,
I figured we could be smooth.
I was in my new life,
And it looked like you brought yours home for the holiday.
But seeing you was enough to twist the knife in my gut.
I didn't need your cordialness.
I didn't need your civility.
At some point you can no longer feel bad
about wearing brass on your knuckles,
and having a bite that can break skin.
So I didn't.
And instead of returning your smile and wave
with one of my own,
I drew blood from your soul
and headed for home.

BITE MARKS

You bite down so hard on your words
that you crack your crooked teeth.
I try my best not to let them sink into me,
but my skin's always been soft.
I replay them on Tuesdays and let them fill me with
dread.
In a second I remember what your arm feels like
when it's snaked around my waist.
I bend backwards and let you inhale me
while I scan your face for any indication
of your future and where I'll be in it.
You tell me "I can't do this"
and defeat tastes like misery and seventeen all over again.
There's no other way to put it,
So I'll let my bones do the talking.
And when they speak of the wind and how it sings through their
holes,
I'll clap as you dance and
rock
while you
roll.

EMPTIED OCEANS

I would like to drink you
the way morning glories drink the dawn,
with little expectation on the rest of the day.
In the places I've come to love the most,
I seem to find a lot of you.
You hang on my walls like those watercolor paintings
I used to love to stare at.
And even in the places I've left,
I think it's fair enough to say you came along with me.
I do my best writing to you in the bathtub,
midday when I should be taking care of more important things.
But that's not how my fingers work,
that's not how my heart beats.
I've learned not to question what it takes to make me heal.
I've learned to expect to live out my days
with you tediously knocking on my chest,
or sending me updates with your new address,
Christmas cards and save the dates.
Maybe I should hate you for the things I craved that you gave to
someone else,
but I'd rather not be the one with the baggage
or the luxury of having to owe you anything.

THE FUTURE WITH(OUT) YOU

Please let me gift you the life in these veins,
it's the least I can do.
Bleached fingers to match a stained heart,
you let me brine in everything we aren't.
We're all just trying to dye what no longer looks like it used to.
I spend the mornings drifting,
and I'm getting pretty good at it.
You should see how well I'm doing now,
I promise you wouldn't even recognize
the skin stretched over my bones.
Sometimes I catch myself stalling,
slowing down too much.
I remind myself that even the grass needs time to sleep,
and I honor a break for a day or two,
then it's right back to dipping my toes in the sand
of you.
You stick all over me even when I wish you were gone.
You tell me how much you love your life now,
yet you're still visiting me on long holiday weekends,
the kind where you leave the city and plan a trip around what I'll be
doing.
I wait by the windows,
glancing at every car that passes.
Not much has changed then,
and I let my lips chap and fingers prune.
If I get lucky and you show,
      we'll spend the first few hours trying to remember how to bleed
      around each other,
      and the last of our time swearing we can't do this ever again.

RUSTED TONGUE

I wake up to find you fresh on my tongue
and I bite my cheek trying to roll over.
In dreams, you are like the wolves I fall asleep next to,
your voice is loose and leaving,
and you run in packs through the corners of my mind.
I untie myself from the headboard,
dig deeper into my morning routine,
and try to decide why I slept with thoughts of you.
I spill my fresh memories onto paper before I step outside,
and prepare myself to let go of you
the way the trees let go of leaves.
I hate that you have sunk into all the places I love.
The water and the rocks are mine,
but I keep finding you skipping them
across the shallow lakes near my heart.
You've stained every freckle
with your deep-water demeanor,
and I wish I could remove all traces of you.
I pass the time slowly with a tongue sharp for cutting
and knees built for running.
It's times like now and later,
when I wonder why you creep into my mind,
settle down, and stay a while.
You were meant to tarnish someone else's rust.
But here you are polishing mine.

SHALLOWS AND DEPTHS

I find you in the shallows
where the roots have no claim,
and the ground is too dry for digging.
My shoes leave traces of where I've been,
there's no escaping this now.
There's never any escaping you.
I tuck you in between
my Sunday best,
and my jewelry that rests
on the bedside table.
You're my five-carat tragedy and
two pounds of gold
that I couldn't sell if I wanted to.
No one pockets you
the way that
I do.
You sift for a better day
despite the lack of sun
and the puddles of rain,
and my heart is still the driest place on Earth.
I carry you around in a
five-gallon bucket
that ends up being too heavy for me to lift at all.
I pour some of you out,
and let you stain the surface of this place
with more sugar than water.

THE LAST TIME

You are golden and frozen,
a perfect mix of all the things undesirable in this world.
I kick up the snow with a little more force
than necessary,
but you don't seem to notice.
I'm left with frostbitten toes
and a chill I can't get rid of.
The world grew quiet when you stopped talking,
but silence is sometimes envied,
although now that's not the case.
I forgot the way you sound when you wrap your tongue
around vowels,
and speak in soft syllables that sleep next to shame.
I crave the timbre of your voice
crooning over youth and our ability to trap it.
I attach myself to you,
like a mechanical valve,
and I beat and beg you to keep breathing,
even if it's not
for me.
You rattle your way across my skin
and leave when you find that you can breathe on your own.
I clamber around the voids of your hotel room,
empty the suitcases and decide to stay
until I figure out what I want to do with the
rest of my life.

A LETTER FROM THE AUTHOR:

I wrote these words and put them into a black notebook starting circa 2004. Initially, I wanted to be a songwriter, but when I realized I had a terrible voice and things really don't turn out like the movie *Coyote Ugly,* I stopped writing in verse and started writing however it felt right. The result was a notebook full of snippets of my life that I hung onto. The deepest part of this collection came in the 2005 - 2008 era, and it comes from the heart of a girl I don't know anymore. When I wrote these, I really thought I'd never get over the way that first loss of love guts you, but now I realize that you have to experience the deep blue melancholy of loss to appreciate what you will gain later.

There's a lot of me inside of this collection, and a lot of other people, as well. My best friend from high school lives amongst some of these pages and the boy who couldn't remember my family member's name and often referred to her as "Margo" is in here, too. Beyond that, there's an abundance of people my roots have grown away from, and sometimes that is a very good thing. Trust me. But if I'm being honest, most of this collection is about me, and all the things I've kept to myself until now.

If you have read this collection and found something inside of it that reminds you of your youth, I'd love to hear about it. There's nothing more therapeutic than hearing someone else's tales of loss, and bonding over it. Loss brings gain, in some way...always.

Never settle, never let someone make you feel like a doormat, and above all else, never be afraid to love.

Xox,

Hayley

You can find more of Hayley Stumbo's books on Amazon! Other works include,

Hide and Seek Her
Finders Keep Her
Every Pane of Glass

Interact with Hayley on social media!
Instagram.com/Haystumbo
Facebook.com.HBStumbo

Visit Hayley's website at hbstumbowrites.com.

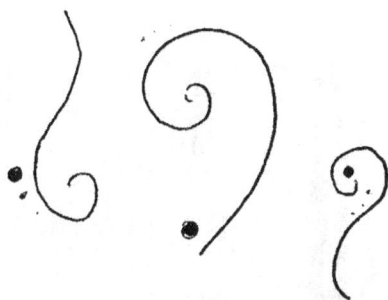

I am the mountain range
inside your heart.

But I am nothing worth
Climbing.

8/8/17

SANTA MONICA

There isn't even
to talk about.

you'll be too far

You'll collapse at the thought of and
I'll carry you to bed.

www.ingramcontent.com/pod-product-compliance
Lightning Source LLC
Chambersburg PA
CBHW020558030426
42337CB00013B/1135